THE
DOG LOVER'S
TREASURY

THE

DOG LOVER'S
TREASURY

Witty and enjoyable writings in praise of dogs

Compiled by Caroline Foley

Capella

DEDICATION:

*For Theo, the little dog
with the heart of a lion.*

This edition published in 2008
by Arcturus Publishing Limited
26/27 Bickels Yard, 151–153 Bermondsey Street,
London SE1 3HA

In Canada published for Indigo Books
468 King St W,
Suite 500,
Toronto,
Ontario M5V 1L8

ISBN: 978-1-84193-840-0

Printed in China

Contents

Introduction

It takes a leap of the imagination to accept that our beloved pets are the descendants of that monster of myth, folklore, legend and fairy tale, the man-eating grey wolf *Canis lupus*. The most likely explanation for this evident domestication is that the prehistoric hunter-gatherer started the process by selectively breeding from wolf cubs so that, over the years, we have developed a truly kaleidoscopic range of breeds.

Present-day dogs vary greatly in size and form, ranging from the pocket-sized Chihuahua to the lofty Great Dane. Their coats come in many colours and patterns and can be smooth, curly, straight, wiry or silky.

They have also been bred to have temperaments that suit particular purposes. So there are dogs that fight, retrieve, rescue, race, catch rabbits, haul in fishing nets, hunt, guide, sniff out, warn, guard, protect – and, of course, act as gentle companions.

In order to reflect this rich diversity, the contents of this volume have been arranged into different categories. Beginning with eulogies to the manicured *Adored Pets* on their silken cushions, we move on to *Dogs with Personality*. Here the spaniel Beau answers back to his master in William Cowper's 18th-century poem and Montmorency, the uncontrollable

'Now thou art dead, no eye shall ever see
For shape and service spaniel like to thee.
This shall my love do. Give thy sad death one
Tear that deserves of me a million.'

ROBERT HERRICK

The Tearaway (1884)
FRANK PATON
(1856–1909)

Brave French Dog in War (1917)
RENÉ PREJELAN
(1877–1968)

fox terrier, gets his comeuppance from a very cool cat in *Three Men in a Boat*.

Next come *Working Dogs*, creatures that labour nobly for mankind. Among them can be found the St Bernard rescue dog, the woodman's companion and even the circus performer.

Dogs at War are the ultimate heroes. One was the stray, Sergeant Stubby, who served in many campaigns and captured an enemy spy single-handed. Another was Airedale Jack, mortally wounded whilst delivering the message that saved his battalion.

No collection would be complete without a villain: in *Legendary Dogs* we come across vicious Bill Sikes and the wretched Bull's-eye. By contrast, there is the touching story of Greyfriars Bobby, the little dog that watched over his master's grave for 14 years.

In the final section, *In Memoriam*, writers like Alexander Pope and Elizabeth Barrett Browning are eloquent in their tributes to their cherished friends, reminding us all of our debt of gratitude to our bright-eyed and much-loved companions.

'The more I see of men, the more I like my dog.'

FREDERICK THE GREAT

A King Charles Spaniel on a Green Cushion (1847)
FERDINAND KRUMHOLZ
(1810–78)

Adored Pets

Epigram engraved on the collar of a dog given to King George II in 1738:

I am his Highness' dog at Kew
Pray, tell me sir, whose dog are you?
ALEXANDER POPE

If Jonathan Swift is being somewhat ironic with his fulsome *Advice to a Dog Painter*, Julian Grenfell is undoubtedly sincere in his admiration for the black greyhound that was as graceful as the 'swallow's flight' and swift as a 'driven hurricane'. Anatole France's puppy, Riquet, disarms the unsuspecting M. Bergeret. Thomas Hardy's Wessex is entirely confident in being 'a popular personage' with the folk he 'lets' live with him. Lord Byron remarks that it is 'sweet to know' that 'an eye will mark' his arrival, and 'look brighter' when he comes. And an anonymous writer is so comforted by his dog after a hard day that he forgets his troubles entirely.

Advice to a Dog Painter

by JONATHAN SWIFT (1667–1745)

Happiest of the spaniel race,

Painter, with thy colours grace,

Draw his forehead large and high,

Draw his blue and humid eye;

Draw his neck so smooth and round,

Little neck with ribands bound;

And the musely swelling breast

Where the Loves and Graces rest;

And the spreading, even back,

Soft, and sleek, and glossy black;

And the tail that gently twines,

Like the tendrils of the vines;

And the silky twisted hair,

Shadowing thick the velvet ear;

Velvet ears which, hanging low,

O'er the veiny temples grow.

Courbet au Chien Noir
(Self-Portrait with Black Dog)
(1842)
GUSTAVE COURBET (1819–77)

To a Greyhound

by JULIAN GRENFELL (1888–1915)

Shining black in the shining light,
Inky black in the golden sun,
Graceful as the swallow's flight,
Light as swallow, wingèd one,
Swift as driven hurricane –
Double-sinewed stretch and spring,
Muffled thud of flying feet,
See the black dog galloping,
Hear his wild foot-beat.

See him lie when the day is dead,
Black curves curled on the boarded floor,
Sleepy eyes, my sleepy-head –
Eyes that were aflame before.
Gentle now they burn no more;
Gentle now and softly warm,
With the fire that made them bright
Hidden – as when after storm
Softly falls the night.

God of speed, who makes the fire –

God of Peace, who lulls the same –

God who gives the fierce desire,

Lust for blood as fierce as flame –

God who stands in Pity's name –

Many may ye be or less,

Ye who rule the earth and sun:

Gods of strength and gentleness,

Ye are ever one.

Hare Coursing in a Landscape (1870)
JOHN MARSHALL (*fl.* 1840–96)

From Riquet's Arrival

by ANATOLE FRANCE (1844–1924)

Seated at his table one morning in front of the window, against which the leaves of the plane tree quivered, M. Bergeret, who was trying to discover how the ships of Aeneas had been changed into nymphs, heard a tap at the door, and forthwith his servant entered, carrying in front of her, opossum-like, a TINY CREATURE whose black head peeped out from the folds of her apron, which she had turned up to form a pocket. With a look of anxiety and hope upon her face she remained motionless for a moment, then she placed the little thing upon the carpet at her master's feet.

'*What's that?*' asked M. Bergeret.

It was a little dog of doubtful breed, having something of the terrier in him, and a well-set head, a short, smooth coat of a dark tan colour, and a tiny little stump of a tail. His body retained its puppy-like softness, and he went sniffling at the carpet.

'*Angélique,*' said M. Bergeret, '*take this animal back to its owner.*'

The Tearaway (1884)
FRANK PATON
(1856–1909)

'*It has no owner, Monsieur.*'

M. Bergeret looked silently at the little creature, who had come to examine his slippers, and was giving little sniffs of approval. M. Bergeret was a philologist, which perhaps explains why at this juncture he asked a vain question.

'*What is he called?*'

'*Monsieur,*' replied Angélique, '*he has no name.*'

M. Bergeret seemed put out by the answer: he looked at the dog sadly, with a disheartened air.

Then the little animal placed its two front paws on M. Bergeret's slipper, and, holding it thus, began innocently to nibble at it. With a sudden excess of compassion M. Bergeret took the tiny nameless creature on his knee. The dog looked at him intently, and M. Bergeret was pleased at his confiding expression.

'*What beautiful eyes!*' he cried.

The dog's eyes were indeed beautiful, the pupils of a golden-flecked chestnut set in warm white. And HIS GAZE SPOKE OF SIMPLE MYSTERIOUS THOUGHTS, common alike to the thoughtful beasts and simple men of the earth.

Tired, perhaps, with the intellectual effort he had made for the purpose of entering into communication with a human being, he closed his beautiful eyes and, yawning widely, revealed his pink mouth, his curled up tongue, and his array of dazzling teeth.

M. Bergeret put his hand into the dog's mouth, and allowed him to lick it, at which old Angélique gave a smile of relief.

'*It was a little dog of doubtful breed, having something of the terrier in him*'

Bulldog (1898)
CECIL CHARLES WINDSOR ALDIN
(1870–1935)

A Popular Personage at Home

by THOMAS HARDY (1840–1928)

'I live here: "Wessex" is my name:
I am a dog known rather well:
I guard the house; but how
   that came
To be my whim I cannot tell.

'With a leap and a heart elate I go
At the end of an hour's expectancy
To take a walk of a mile or so
With the folk I let live here
   with me.

'Along the path, amid the grass
I sniff, and find out rarest smells
For rolling over as I pass
The open fields towards the dells.

'No doubt I shall always cross
   this sill,

And turn the corner, and
   stand steady,
And gazing back for my
   mistress till
She reaches where I have
   run already.

'And that this meadow with
   its brook,
And bulrush, even as it appears
As I plunge by with hasty look,
Will stay the same a
   thousand years.'

Thus 'Wessex'. But a dubious ray
At times informs his steadfast eye,
Just for a trice, as though to say,
'Yet this will pass, and pass shall I?'

A Pointer (1905)
Arthur Wardle
(1864–1949)

The Dog and the Waterlily

by WILLIAM COWPER (1731–1800)

The noon was shady, and soft airs
Swept Ouse's silent tide,
When 'scap'd from literary cares,
I wander'd on his side.

My spaniel, prettiest of his race,
And high in pedigree –
(Two nymphs adorn'd with every grace
That spaniel found for me,)

Now wanton'd lost in flags and reeds,
Now, starting into sight,
Pursued the swallow o'er the meads
With scarce a slower flight.

It was the time when Ouse display'd,
His lilies newly blown;
Their beauties I intent survey'd
And one I wish'd my own.

A King Charles Spaniel (1792)
WILLIAM ELLIS (1747–1810)

With cane extended far I sought
To steer it close to land;
But still the prize, though
  nearly caught,
Escaped my eager hand.

Beau mark'd my unsuccessful pains
With fix'd considerate face,
And puzzling set his puppy brains
To comprehend the case.

But with a cherup clear and strong
Dispersing all his dream,
I thence withdrew, and
  follow'd long
The windings of the stream.

My ramble ended, I return'd,
Beau, trotting far before,
The floating wreath
  again discern'd,
And plunging left the shore.

I saw him with that lily cropp'd
Impatient swim to meet
My quick approach, and soon
  he dropp'd
The treasure at my feet.

Charm'd with the sight, 'The
  world,' I cried,
'Shall hear of this thy deed;
My dog shall mortify the pride
Of man's superior breed;

'But chief myself I will enjoin,
Awake at duty's call,
To show a love as prompt as thine
To Him who gives me all.'

Study of Clumber Spaniel in
Wooded River Landscape (1807)
EDWARD COOPER
(*fl.*1803–31)

My Comforter

ANONYMOUS

The world had all gone wrong that day
And tired and in despair
Discouraged with the ways of life,
I sank into my chair.

A soft caress fell on my cheek,
My hands were thrust apart,
And two big sympathizing eyes
Gazed down into my heart.

I had a friend; what cared I now
For fifty worlds? I knew
One heart was anxious when I grieved –
My dog's heart, loyal, true.

'God bless him,' breathed I soft and low,
And hugged him close and tight,
One lingering lick upon my ear
And we were happy – quite.

There's No Place Like Home (1853)
SIR EDWIN HENRY LANDSEER
(1802–73)

A Friendly Welcome (1818)

by GEORGE GORDON, LORD BYRON

(1788–1824)

'Tis sweet to hear the watch-dog's honest bark

Bay deep-mouthed welcome as we draw near home;

'Tis sweet to know there is an eye will mark

Our coming, and look brighter when we come.

On Tiger's Collar (*c.*1728)

by JONATHAN SWIFT (1667–1745)

Pray steal me not; I'm Mrs. Dingley's,

Whose heart in this four-footed thing lies.

Will He Come Back? (1888)
ROBERT MORLEY
(1857–1941)

Dogs with Personality

*The great pleasure of a dog is that you may make a fool of yourself with him
and not only will he not scold you, but he will make a fool of himself too.*
Samuel Butler

Here we meet Jerome K. Jerome's Montmorency, the dog
that caused the writer to remark that fox terriers had
four times more original sin in them than other dogs;
D.H. Lawrence's Bibbles, the exuberant black 'dragon' dog
with the 'Chinese puzzle face' that liked to chase coyotes
that could swallow him 'like an oyster' and 'pelt the dusty
trail' after horses; and Rupert Brookes' small dog that
went berserk one day and 'shammed furious rabies, and
bit all the babies...' among other unspeakable crimes. Then
there is Don Marquis' puppy, who disgraced himself in
front of his mistress' tea party guests having somewhat
over-indulged all day.

Bulldog (1927)
Cecil Charles Aldin
(1870–1935)

From Three Men in a Boat (1889)
by JEROME K. JEROME (1859–1927)

O*ne day the naughty fox terrier Montmorency, having stirred up a dog fight, saw a cat trotting across the High Street. With a cry of joy he flew after his prey; a large, black, disreputable-looking tomcat. It was a long, sinewy-looking animal with a calm, contented look about it, though it only had half a tail, a chewed nose and one ear...*

... MONTMORENCY went for the poor cat at about twenty miles an hour; but the cat did not hurry up, did not seem to have grasped the idea that its life was in danger. It trotted quietly on until its would-be assassin was within a yard of it, and then it turned round and sat down in the middle of the road, and looked at Montmorency with a gentle inquiring expression, that said:

'*Yes, you want me?*'

Montmorency does not lack pluck; but there was something about the look of that cat that might have chilled the heart of the boldest dog. He stopped abruptly and LOOKED BACK AT TOM.

Fox Terrier with the Day's Bag
ENGLISH SCHOOL (19th century)

Neither spoke; but the conversation that one could imagine was clearly as follows:

The Cat: *'Can I do anything for you?'*

Montmorency: *'No – no thanks.'*

The Cat: *'Don't mind speaking, if you really want anything you know.'*

Montmorency (backing down the High Street): *'Oh no – not at all – certainly don't you trouble. I – I am afraid I've made a mistake. I thought I knew you. Sorry I disturbed you.'*

The Cat: *'Not at all – quite a pleasure. Sure you don't want anything, now?'*

Montmorency (still backing): *'Not at all thanks – not at all – very kind of you. Good morning.'*

THEN THE CAT ROSE, and continued his trot; and Montmorency, fitting what he calls his tail carefully into its groove, came back to us, and took up an unimportant position in the rear.

To this day, if you say the word 'CATS!' to Montmorency, he will visibly shrink and look up piteously at you as if to say:

'Please don't.'

Waiting for Master (1907)
GEORGE PAICE
(1845–1925)

'To this day, if you say the word "CATS!" to Montmorency, he will visibly shrink and look up piteously at you as if to say: "Please don't."'

From Bibbles (*c.*1923)

by D.H. LAWRENCE (1885–1930)

… Oh Bibbles, oh Pips, oh Pipsey,
You little black love-bird!
Don't you love *everybody*!
Just everybody.
You love 'em all.
Believe in the One Identity,
   don't you,
You little Walt–Whitmanesque
   bitch?
First time I lost you in Taos plaza,
And found you after
   endless chasing,
Came upon you prancing around a
   corner in exuberant
   bibbling affection

After the black-green skirts of
   a yellow-green old
   Mexican woman
Who hated you, and kept looking
   round at you and cursing you in
   a mutter,
While you pranced and bounced
   with love of her, you
   indiscriminating animal,
All your wrinkled *miserere*
   Chinese black little face beaming
And your black little body
   bouncing and wriggling
With indiscriminate love, Bibbles;
I had a moment of pure detestation
   of you…

Yet you're so nice,

So quick, like a little black dragon.

So fierce, when the coyotes howl,

    barking like a whole little lion,

    and rumbling,

And starting forward in the dusk,

    with your little black fur all

    bristling like plush

Against those coyotes, who would

rather swallow you like an oyster.

And in the morning, when the

    bedroom door is opened,

Rushing in like a little black

    whirlwind, leaping straight as an

    arrow on the bed at the pillow

And turning the day suddenly into

    a black tornado of joie de vivre,

    Chinese dragon.

Dog (1902)
HENRI GAUDIER-BRZESKA
(1891–1915)

So funny

Lobbing wildly through deep snow
like a rabbit,

Hurtling like a black ball through
the snow,

Champing it, tossing a mouthful,

Little black spot in the landscape!

So absurd

Pelting behind on the dusty trail
when the horse sets off home at
a gallop:

Left in the dust behind like a dust
ball tearing along,

Coming up on fierce little legs,
tearing fast to catch up, a real
little dust-pig, ears almost
blown away,

And black eyes bulging bright in
a dust-mask

Chinese-dragon-wrinkled, with a
pink mouth grinning, under a
jaw shoved out

And white teeth showing in your
dragon-grin as you race, you
split face,

Like a trundling projectile swiftly
whirling up...

Plenty of conceit in you.

Unblemished belief in your

  own perfection

And utter lovableness, you

  ugly mug;

Chinese puzzle-face,

Wrinkled underhung physiog that

  looks as if it had done

  with everything,

Through with everything.

Instead of which you sit there and

  roll your head like a canary

And show a tiny bunch of

  white teeth in your

  underhung blackness,

Self-conscious little bitch,

Aiming again at being loved…

*A King Charles Spaniel Seated on
a Red Cushion (1834)*
EUGENE JOSEPH VERBOECKHOVEN
(1798–1881)

The Little Dog's Day

by RUPERT BROOKE (1887–1915)

All in the town were still asleep,
When the sun came up with a shout and a leap.
In the lonely streets unseen by man,
A little dog danced. And the day began.

All his life he'd been good, as far as he could,
And the poor little beast had done all that he should.
But this morning he swore, by Odin and Thor
And the canine Valhalla – he'd stand it no more!

So his prayer he got granted – to do just what
    he wanted
Prevented by none, for the space of one day.
'*Iam incipiebo, sedere facebo,*'
In dog-Latin he quoth, '*Euge! sophos! Hurray!*'
He fought with the he-dogs and winked at
    the she-dogs.

The Bone of Contention (1857)
GEORGE ARMFIELD *(after* J.F. HERRING*)*
(c. 1808–93*)*

A thing that had never been heard of before.

'For the stigma of gluttony, I care not a button!' he

Cried, and ate all he could swallow – and more.

He took sinewy lumps from the shins of old frumps,

And mangled the errand boys – when he could get 'em!

He shammed furious rabies, and bit all the babies,

And followed the cats up the trees, and then ate 'em!

They thought 'twas the devil was holding a revel.

And sent for the parson to drive him away;

For the town never knew such a hullabaloo

As that little dog raised – till the end of that day.

When the blood-red sun had gone burning down,

And the lights were lit in the little town,

Outside in the gloom of the twilight grey,

The little dog died when he'd had his day.

Spilt Milk (1892)
PHILIP EUSTACE STRETTON
(died *c.* 1915)

On a Spaniel called Beau Killing a Young Bird (1793)

by WILLIAM COWPER (1731–1800)

A spaniel Beau, that fares like you,
Well fed, and at his ease,
Should wiser be, than to pursue
Each trifle that he sees.

But you have kill'd a tiny bird,
Which flew not till to-day,
Against my orders, whom you heard
Forbidding you the prey.

Nor did you kill, that you might eat,
And ease a doggish pain,
For him, though chas'd with
   furious heat,
You left where he was slain.

Nor was he of the thievish sort,
Or one whom blood allures,
But innocent was all his sport,
Whom you have torn for yours.

My dog! What remedy remains,
Since, teach you all I can,
I see you, after all my pains
So much resemble man!

Le Chien Barbet (The Spaniel) (1730)
PRIVATE COLLECTION

BEAU'S REPLY

Sir! when I flew to seize the bird,
In spite of your command,
A louder voice than yours I heard
The harder to withstand:

Your cried – Forbear! – but in
    my breast
A mightier cried – Proceed!
'Twas Nature, Sir, whose
    strong behest
Impell'd me to the deed.

Yet such as nature I respect,
I ventur'd once to break
(As you perhaps may recollect)
Her precept for your sake;

As when your linnet, on a day,
Passing his prison door,
Had flutter'd all his strength away,
And panting press'd the floor,

Well knowing him a sacred thing,
Not destin'd to my tooth,
I only kiss'd his ruffled wing,
And lick'd the feathers smooth.

Let my obedience then excuse
My disobedience now,
Nor some reproof yourself refuse
From your aggriev'd Bow-wow!

If killing birds be such a crime,
(Which I can hardly see)
What think you, Sir, of
    killing Time
With verse address'd to me?

Portrait of a Spaniel (1843)
ZACHARIAS NOTERMAN
(1813–74)

From His Apologies (1910)

by RUDYARD KIPLING (1865–1936)

Master, this is Thy Servant. He is rising eight
weeks old.

He is mainly Head and Tummy. His legs
are uncontrolled.

But Thou hast forgiven his ugliness, and
settled him on Thy knee...

Art Thou content with Thy Servant? He
is very comfy with Thee.

Master, behold a Sinner! He hath committed a wrong.

He hath defiled Thy Premises through being kept in
too long.

Wherefore his nose has been rubbed in the dirt and his
self-respect has been bruised.

Master, pardon Thy Sinner, and see he is
properly loosed.

Master, again Thy Sinner! This that was once Thy Shoe,

He has found and taken and carried aside, as fitting
matter to chew.

Mischievous Puppy (1896)
CECIL CHARLES WINDSOR ALDIN
(1870–1935)

Now there is neither blacking nor tongue, and the
    Housemaid has us in tow,
Master, remember Thy Servant is young, and tell her to
    let him go!

Master, extol Thy Servant, he has met a most
    Worthy Foe!
There has been fighting all over the Shop – and into
    the Shop also!
Till cruel umbrellas parted the strife (or I might have
    been choking him yet),
But Thy Servant has had the Time of his Life – and
    now shall we call on the vet?

Master, behold Thy Servant! Strange children came
to play,
And because they fought to caress him, Thy Servant
    wentedst away.
But now that the Little Beasts have gone, he has
    returned to see

(Brushed – with his Sunday collar on) what they left
    over from tea…

Give A Dog A Bone (1888)
WILLIAM HENRY HAMILTON TROOD
(1860–99)

From The Twa Dogs (1786)
by ROBERT BURNS (1759–96)

'Twas in that place o' Scotland's isle,
    That bears the name o' auld King Coil,
Upon a bonie day in June,
When wearin' thro' the afternoon,
Twa dogs, that were na thrang at hame,
Forgather'd ance upon a time.

The first I'll name, they ca'd him Caesar,
Was keepit for His Honor's pleasure:
His hair, his size, his mouth, his lugs,
Shew'd he was nane o' Scotland's dogs;
But whalpit some place far abroad,
Whare sailors gang to fish for cod.

His locked, letter'd, braw brass collar
Shew'd him the gentleman an' scholar;
But though he was o' high degree,
The fient a pride, nae pride had he;
But wad hae spent an hour caressin,
Ev'n wi' al tinkler-gipsy's messin:

Twa Dogs (1858)
SIR EDWIN HENRY LANDSEER
(1802–73)

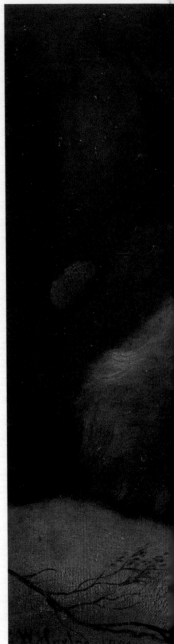

At kirk or market, mill or smiddie,

Nae tawted tyke, tho' e'er sae duddie,

But he wad stan't, as glad to see him,

An' stroan't on stanes an' hillocks wi' him.

The tither was a ploughman's collie –

A rhyming, ranting, raving billie,

Wha for his friend an' comrade had him,

And in freak had Luath ca'd him,

After some dog in Highland Sang

Was made lang syne – Lord knows how lang.

He was a gash an' faithfu' tyke,

As ever lap a sheugh or dyke.

His honest, sonsie, baws'nt face

Aye gat him friends in ilka place;

His breast was white, his touzie back

Weel clad wi' coat o' glossy black;

His gawsie tail, wi' upward curl,

Hung owre his hurdie's wi' a swirl.

The Lords of the Isles (1881)
GEORGE W. HORLOR *(fl. 1849–91)*

From 'On an Amateur Beat'

in The Uncommercial Traveller (1859)
by CHARLES DICKENS (1812–70)

Between 1860 and 1869, Charles Dickens wrote a series of articles about London life, which appeared in the journal All the Year Round. *The pieces were later included in* The Uncommercial Traveller. *In 'A Small Star in the East' and 'On an Amateur Beat' we meet Poodles, a mongrel found starving outside The Children's Hospital in the East End of London. Poodles was to become something of a celebrity in the hospital, as he cheered up the children with his comical ways. His collar, given to him by 'An admirer of his mental endowments', was inscribed with the words 'Judge not Poodles by external appearances'.*

'… I find him (Poodles) making the round of the beds, like a house-surgeon, attended by another dog… who appears to trot about with him in the character of his pupil dresser. POODLES is anxious to make me known to a pretty little girl looking wonderfully healthy, who had had a leg taken off for cancer of the knee. A difficult operation, Poodles intimates, WAGGING HIS TAIL on the counterpane, but perfectly successful, as you see, dear sir! The patient, patting Poodles, adds with a smile, '*The leg was so much trouble to me, that I am glad it's gone.*' I never saw anything in doggery finer than the deportment of

Poodles, when another little girl opens her mouth to show
a peculiar enlargement of the tongue. Poodles (at that
time on a table, to be on a level with the occasion) looks
at the tongue (with his own sympathetically out) so very
gravely and knowingly, that I feel inclined to put my hand
in my waistcoat-pocket, and give him a guinea, wrapped
in paper...'

Häusliche Toilette (1655)
BARTOLOMÉ ESTÉBAN MURILLO
(1618-82)

Confessions of a Glutton

by DON MARQUIS (1878–1937)

After I ate my dinner then I ate
part of a shoe

i found some archies by a bathroom pipe

and ate them too

i ate some glue

i ate a bone that had got nice and ripe

six weeks buried in the ground

i ate a little mousie that I found

i ate some sawdust from the cellar floor

it tasted sweet

i ate some outcast meat

and some roach paste by the pantry door

and then the missis had some folks to tea

nice folks who petted me

and so I ate

cakes from a plate

i ate some polish that they use

for boots and shoes

and then I went back to the missis swell tea party

After a Hard Day's Hunting (1892)
ARTHUR WARDLE
(1864–1949)

i guess I must have eat too hearty

of something maybe cake

for then came the earthquake

you should have seen the missis face

and when the boss came in she said

no wonder that dog hangs his head

he knows hes in disgrace

i am a well intentioned little pup

but sometimes things come up

to get a little dog in bad

and now I feel so very sad

but the boss said never mind old scout

time wears disgraces out.

Confrontation (1883)
ALFRED DUKE
(died *c*.1905)

Working Dogs

Of all the animals that have been domesticated by man, dogs can perhaps claim the largest array of natural talents. It is difficult to imagine what the world would have been like without the benefit of their astonishing versatility. If we began to make a list of the many ways in which dogs assist mankind it would soon include herding, droving, pulling carts and sledges, hauling, hunting, retrieving, racing, scenting, rescuing, guarding and fighting. We could go on to include guide dogs for the blind and the deaf, and dogs working as actors in film and television productions and as sniffer dogs for the K9 (canine) police and customs units. This part of the book celebrates the lives of working dogs everywhere.

Dogs and Hunting Gear (1775)
FRANCISCO JOSÉ DE GOYA Y LUCIENTES
(1746–1828)

The Properties of a Good Greyhound

by JULIANA BERNERS (b.1388)

A greyhound should be headed like a Snake,
And necked like a Drake,
Footed like a Cat,
Tailed like a Rat,
Sidèd like a Team,
Chined like a Beam.

The first year he must learn to feed,
The second year to field him lead,
The third year he is fellow-like,
The fourth year there is none sike,
The fifth year he is good enough,
The sixth year he shall hold the plough,
The seventh year he will avail
Great bitches for to assail,
The eighth year lick ladle,
The ninth year cart saddle,
And when he is comen to that year
Have him to the tanner,
For the best hound that ever bitch had
At nine year he is full bad.

From the fresco of
Diana and Actaeon
FRANCESCO MAZZOLA
PARMIGIANINO (1503–40)

Barry, the Saint Bernard

by SAMUEL ROGERS (1763–1855)

When the storm
Rose, and the snow rolled on in ocean-waves,
When on his face the experienced traveller fell,
Sheltering his lips and nostrils with his hands,
Then all was changed; and, sallying with their pack
Into that blank of nature, they became
Unearthly beings. 'Anselm, higher up,
Just where it drifts, a dog howls loud and long,
And now, as guided by a voice from Heaven,
Digs with his feet. That noble vehemence,
Whose can it be, but his who never erred?
A man lies underneath! Let us to work.'

A St Bernard (1877)
HEINRICH SPERLING
(1844–1924)

Hare Coursing (1805)

from **Incident Characteristic of a Favourite Dog**

by **WILLIAM WORDSWORTH (1770–1850)**

On his morning rounds the Master
Goes to learn how all things fare;
Searches pasture after pasture,
Sheep and cattle eyes with care;
And, for silence or for talk,
He hath comrades in his walk;
Four dogs, each pair a different breed,
Distinguished two for scent and two for speed.

See a hare before him started!
Off they fly in earnest chase;
Every dog is eager-hearted,
All the four are in the race:
And the hare whom they pursue,
Knows from instinct what to do;
Her hope is near: no turn she makes;
But like an arrow to the river takes. ...

The Slipper (1812)
ABRAHAM COOPER
(1787–1868)

The Woodman's Dog

from **The Task** (1785)

by **WILLIAM COWPER** (1731–1800)

Forth goes the woodman, leaving unconcern'd
The cheerful haunts of man; to wield the axe
And drive the wedge, in yonder forest drear,
From morn to eve his solitary task.
Shaggy, and lean, and shrewd, with pointed ears
And tail cropp'd short, half lurcher and half cur —
His dog attends him. Close behind his heel
Now creeps he slow; and now, with many a frisk
Wide-scamp'ring, snatches up the drifted snow
With iv'ry teeth, or ploughs it with his snout;
Then shakes his powder'd coat, and barks for joy.

Shepherd Guarding his Flock of Sheep,
Baden Province (19th century)

Fidelity of the Dog (*c.*1805)

by WILLIAM WORDSWORTH (1770–1850)

A barking sound the shepherd hears,
A cry as of a dog or fox;
He halts, and searches with his eyes
Among the scattered rocks:
And now at distance can discern
A stirring in a break of fern;
And instantly a dog is seen,
Glancing through that covert green.

The dog is not of mountain breed;
Its motions are too wild and shy;
With something, as the shepherd thinks,
Unusual in its cry.
Nor is there anyone in sight
All round, in hollow, or on height;
Nor shout, nor whistle, strikes his ear;
What is the creature doing here?

It was a cove, a huge recess,
That keeps till June December's snow;
A lofty precipice in front,
A silent tarn below!
Far in the bosom of Helvellyn,

Detail from *Les Garde-Côtes Gaulois (1882)*
J-J-A LECOMTE NOUY
(1842–1923)

Remote from public road or dwelling,
Pathway of cultivated land,
From trace of human foot or hand.

There sometimes doth a leaping fish
Send through the tarn a lonely cheer;
The crags repeat the raven's croak,
In symphony austere;
Thither the rainbow comes

  – the cloud –

And mists that spread the flying shroud;
And sunbeams, and the sounding blast,
That if it could would hurry past;
But that enormous barrier binds it fast.

Not free from boding thoughts, awhile
The shepherd stood; then makes his way
Towards the dog o'er rocks and stones,
As quickly as he may;
Not far had gone before he found
A human skeleton on the ground;
The appall'd discoverer with a sigh,
Looks round to learn the history.

From those abrupt and perilous rocks
The man had fall'n, that place of fear!

At length upon the shepherd's mind
It breaks and all is clear;
He instantly recalled the name,
And who he was and whence he came;
Remember'd too the very day
On which the traveller pass'd this way.

But hear a wonder, for whose sake
This lamentable tale I tell!
A lasting monument of words
This wonder merits well.
The dog which still was hovering nigh,
Repeating the same timid cry,
This dog had been, through three
  month's space,
A dweller in that savage place.

Yes, proof was plain that since that day
When this ill-fated traveller died,
The dog had watched about the spot,
Or by his master's side:
How nourish'd here through such
  long time,
He knows who gave that love sublime;
And gave that strength of feeling great
Above all human estimate.

A Greyhound in a Hilly Landscape
(1856)
JAMES BEARD (1814–93)

Performing Dogs

from The Old Curiosity Shop (1850)

by CHARLES DICKENS (1812–70)

Little Nell had just arrived at the Jolly Sandboys Inn with her travelling companions when they were interrupted by Jerry and his troupe of canine dancers…

These were no other than FOUR VERY DISMAL DOGS, who came pattering in one after the other, headed by an old bandy dog of particularly mournful aspect, who, stopping when the last of his followers had got as far as the door, erected himself on his hind legs and looked round at his companions, who immediately stood upon their hind legs in a grave and melancholy row. Nor was this the only remarkable circumstance about these dogs, for each of them wore a kind of little coat of some gaudy colour trimmed with tarnished spangles, and one of them had a cap upon his head, tied very carefully under his chin, which had fallen down upon his nose and completely obscured one eye…

From a *Hand and Machine* trade card (*c.*1890)

'...each of them wore a kind of

little coat of some gaudy colour

trimmed with tarnished spangles'

Dogs at War

'They had no choice.'
Inscription on the ANIMALS IN WAR MEMORIAL,
HYDE PARK, LONDON

Dogs have been taken to fight in battles alongside soldiers since early times. Julius Caesar admired the fighting spirit of the English mastiffs during the Roman Conquest of 55BC; they were sent into the fray armed with spiked collars that tore at the legs of the enemy's horses, or with flaming torches designed to terrify them.

In the 20th century, dogs were widely used to signal the approach of the enemy and sniff out ambushes, arms caches and enemy encampments. They could detect mines, give advance warning of invasions and be sent out to find and help wounded soldiers in No Man's Land. Moving some five times faster than a human across difficult terrain, they could often pass as unnoticed as shadows to deliver messages, or even lay short lengths of cable behind them as they went.

I'm Neutral, BUT – Not afraid of any of them (1915)
PRIVATE COLLECTION

Moustache – a French Poodle

THE NAPOLEONIC WARS (1800–1815)

Moustache, a black poodle, was the mascot of the French Grenadiers in the Austrian campaign. He is most famous for attending to the French flag bearer who lay dying in the field. Moustache could do nothing for the flag bearer but gathered the flag up and bore it triumphantly back to his side of the lines.

He was given a tricolor collar bearing the words: '*Moustache, a French dog, a brave fighter entitled to respect.*'

On the other side it read: '*At the Battle of Austerlitz, he had his leg broken while saving the flag of his regiment.*'

Grenadier with Dog (1824)
PIERRE ROCH VIGNERON
(1789–1872)

Napoleon Weeps Over a Dog

THE BATTLE OF MARENGO, JUNE 1800

Napoleon Bonaparte wrote in his memoirs about an incident of A DOG TRYING TO ROUSE HIS DEAD MASTER and when that failed, trying to get Napoleon to come and help.

'This soldier, I realized, must have friends at home and in his regiment; *yet he lay there deserted by all except his dog.* … I had looked on, unmoved, at battles which decided the future of nations. Tearless I had given orders which brought death to thousands. Yet, here was I stirred, profoundly stirred, stirred to tears. And by what? By the grief of one dog…'

Grenadiers in the Snow (1834)
FERDINAND VON RAYSKI
(1806–90)

'I had looked on, unmoved...

Yet, here was I stirred... By the

grief of one dog...'

The Mercy Dogs
THE FIRST WORLD WAR (1914–18)

Mercy dogs were trained to hunt silently for wounded soldiers in NO MAN'S LAND.

Under the cover of night, they would foray in the battlefields for the injured and dying. They were taught to bring back a cap or tear off a small piece of clothing as evidence, and to refresh their memories when they returned with the stretcher bearers. They often carried medical supplies and water. Mercy Dogs saved the lives of thousands of soldiers in the First World War. In 1917, PRUSCO, a French dog, was reported in The Red Cross Magazine as having single-handedly saved more than 100 lives after a battle, even dragging wounded soldiers under cover to protect them.

Soldiers, Horses and Dogs Protected by Gas Masks (1918) ACHILLE BELTRAME (1871–1945)

Sergeant Stubby

FRANCE, 1918

The Good Dog of France – Always the First (1917)
RENÉ PREJELAN
(1877–1968)

SERGEANT STUBBY, a stray smuggled out on the USS *Minnesota* by crew member John Robert Conway, came to serve with the 102nd Infantry, 26th Division in the trenches in France, taking part in four offences and 17 battles. In April 1918 he was wounded in the leg by a hand grenade. After he had been gassed by the enemy, he was able to warn his unit of poisonous gas attacks. He located wounded soldiers in No Man's Land and could give advance warning to the men of artillery fire. He CAPTURED A GERMAN SPY SINGLE-HANDED in the Argonne. When the United States forces took the town of Château Thierry, the grateful women of the town made him a beautiful coat of chamois leather covered in medals.

Airedale Jack

FRANCE, 1918

In the Imperial War Museum in London, there is a plaque inscribed '... *to the memory of Airedale Jack, a hero of the Great War'*. Originally from Battersea Dogs Home, Airedale Jack was trained in the British War Dog School and was sent to the front in France with the Sherwood Foresters. When they were later almost defeated in battle and were cut off on all sides, the only way to get a message through the enemy lines to HQ for reinforcements was to send Airedale Jack. *With a leather pouch on his back, Jack slid through the night keeping low as he'd been taught.* Shrapnel broke his jaw, then a missile ripped his skin open from shoulder to thigh. Still he continued. His front paw was hit but he carried on valiantly, the last few miles on three legs. HE FELL DEAD ON ARRIVAL but he had saved the battalion.

Ricky the Mine Dog

6TH JUNE 1944

Dogs were invaluable as MINE DETECTORS during the Second World War. Four platoons of 29 mine-detecting dogs were sent with the British invasion force after D-Day to help them clear mines as they advanced across Normandy. *The dogs were trained to stop stock still a metre away when they scented a mine and then bark.* Welsh sheepdog Ricky was sent to help his handler Maurice Yelding clear mines along the canal at Nederdent in the Netherlands. Ricky detected three mines at speed. One went off instantly killing the commander. Despite a severe head injury, Ricky led Yelding through the minefield and out of danger.

Detail from *Eugenie Graff (Madame Paul) (1882)*
CLAUDE MONET
(1840–1926)

Man's Best Friend (1807)
CHARLES TOWNE
(1763–1840)

Legendary Dogs

*'… So lay Argos the hound, all shivering with dog-ticks. Yet the instant
Odysseus approached, the beast knew him. He thumped his tail and
drooped his ears forward, but lacked the power to drag himself ever so little
towards his master. However, Odysseus saw him out of the corner of his eye
and brushed away a tear…'*

T.E. LAWRENCE

Homer's Argos, the single creature to recognize and greet
Odysseus after a lifetime's absence, only to die at his feet
upon his return, is one of the earliest and most celebrated
fictional dog heroes in literature. A couple of centuries
later, Aesop provided the world with fables, or moral tales,
such as 'The Dog and the Reflection'. Later in history
comes the story of Beth Gêlert. In the year 1205, King
John reputedly gave him as a wedding gift to the Welsh
prince Llewellyn, who later made a grave error of
judgment when he slew his favourite hound.

But not all dog heroes are fictional. Greyfriars Bobby
was certainly real, but his unswerving fidelity to his master
is surely the stuff of legends.

From Brown Wolf

by JACK LONDON (1876–1916)

Madge and her poet husband Walt Irvine, living in sunny California, TOOK IN
WOLF, A MAGNIFICENT BUT WILD, FEROCIOUS SLEDGE DOG clearly
strayed from the Klondike Gold Rush in Alaska. They fed him and tried to tame
him but as soon as he had the strength, he would run off and travel hundreds of
miles overland heading home to the north. They put on a collar advertising a
reward for his return and frequently paid to have him brought back. In time, their
efforts were rewarded. HE CAME TO TRUST THEM AND SEEMED TO
SETTLE IN. But one day, by purest chance, a stranger by the name of Skiff Miller
came across them on his way to his sister's house and stopped to ask them
directions. When he saw Wolf…

'*Well, I'll be damned!*' he enunciated slowly and solemnly.

He sat down ponderingly on the log and left Madge standing. At the sound of
his voice, Wolf's ears had flattened down, and then his mouth had opened in a
laugh. He trotted slowly up to the stranger and first smelled his hands and then
licked them with his tongue.

Skiff Miller patted the dog's head, and slowly and solemnly repeated, '*Well, I'll
be damned!*'

'*Excuse me, ma'am,*' he said at the next moment '*I just was surprised, that was all.*'

'*We're surprised too,*' she answered lightly. '*We never saw Wolf make up to a
stranger before.*'

'*Is that what you call him – Wolf?*' the man asked.

Madge nodded. '*But I can't understand his friendliness to you – unless it's because
you're from the Klondike. He's a Klondike dog you know.*'

'*Yes'm*,' Miller said absently. He lifted one of Wolf's forelegs and examined the foot-pads, pressing them and denting them with his thumb. '*Kind of soft*,' he remarked. '*He ain't been on trail for a long time.*'

'*I say*,' Walt broke in, '*it is remarkable the way he lets you handle him.*'

Skip Miller arose, no longer awkward with the admiration of Madge, and in a sharp, business-like manner asked, '*How long have you had him?*'

But just then the dog, squirming and rubbing against the

Knud Rasmussen and Sledge Dogs (1921)
HARALD MOLTKE
(1871–1960)

newcomer's legs, opened his mouth and barked. IT WAS AN EXPLOSIVE BARK, BRIEF AND JOYOUS, BUT A BARK.

'*That's a new one on me,*' Skiff Miller remarked.

Walt and Madge looked at each other. The miracle had happened. Wolf had barked.

'*It's the first time he ever barked,*' said Madge.

'*First time I ever heard him, too,*' Miller volunteered.

Madge smiled at him. The man was evidently a humorist.

'*Of course,*' she said, '*since you only seen him for five minutes.*'

Skiff Miller looked at her sharply, seeking in her face the guile her words had led him to suspect.

'*I thought you understood,*' he said slowly. '*I thought you'd tumbled to it from his makin' up to me. He's my dog. His name isn't Wolf, it's Brown.*'…

Skiff Miller turned to the dog. '*Brown!*' His voice rang out sharply, and at the sound the dog's ears flattened down as to a caress. '*Gee!*' The dog made a swinging turn to the right. '*Now, mush on!*' And the dog ceased his swing abruptly and started straight ahead, halting obediently at command.

'*I can do it with whistles,*' Skiff Miller said proudly. '*He was my lead dog.*'

'*But you are not going to take him away with you?*' Madge asked tremulously.

The man nodded.

'*Back into that awful Klondike world of suffering?*'

He nodded and added: '*Oh, it ain't so bad as all that. Look at me. Pretty healthy specimen, ain't I?*'

'*Oh, but the dogs! The terrible hardship, the heartbreaking toil, the starvation, the frost! Oh, I've read about it and I know.*'

'*I nearly ate him once, over on Little Fish River,*' Miller volunteered grimly. '*If I hadn't got a moose that day was all that saved 'm.*'

In the end it is agreed that Wolf Brown will choose whom to stay with. Neither party will give him any signal. Miller walks slowly away without turning around. After dashing from one to the other in an agony of indecision Wolf finally makes up his mind. He turns away from Madge and Walt…

WOLF'S TROT BROKE INTO A RUN. Wider and wider were the leaps he made. Not once did he turn his head, his wolf's brush standing out straight behind him. HE CUT SHARPLY ACROSS THE CURVE OF THE TRAIL AND WAS GONE.

Buck, Sitting on the Porch of Judge Miller's House (1912)
PAUL BRANSOM (1895–1979)

Theseus' Hounds

from A Midsummer Night's Dream (c.1590)
by WILLIAM SHAKESPEARE (1564–1666)

THESEUS:

My hounds are bred out of the Spartan kind,

So flew'd, so sanded; and their heads are hung

With ears that sweep away the morning dew;

Crook-kneed, and dew-lapp'd like Thessalian bulls;

Slow in pursuit, but match'd in mouth like bells,

Each under each. A cry more tuneable

Was never holla'd to, nor cheer'd with horn,

In Crete, in Sparta, nor in Thessaly;

Judge when you hear.

*The Dogs of Ludovico Gonzaga
(15th century)*
ANDREA MANTEGNA
(1431 1506)

Bull's-eye and Bill Sikes

from *Oliver Twist* (1838)
by CHARLES DICKENS (1812–70)

*D*ickens describes Bill Sikes' famously savage dog, Bull's-eye, as prone to 'a
certain malicious licking of his lips' and a tendency to be 'meditating an attack
upon the legs of the first gentleman or lady he might encounter.' Here Sikes
and Bull's-eye meet head on. For no apparent reason, Sikes kicks him across
the room…

… *'Keep quiet, you warmint! Keep quiet!'* said Mr. Sikes,
suddenly breaking silence.

Dogs are not generally apt to revenge injuries inflicted
upon them by their masters; but MR. SIKES' DOG,
HAVING FAULTS IN COMMON WITH HIS OWNER,
and labouring, perhaps, at this moment, under a powerful
sense of injury, made no more ado but at once fixed his
teeth in one of the half boots. Having given it a hearty
shake, he retired, growling, under a form; just escaping the
pewter measure which Mr. Sikes levelled at his head.

'You would, would you?' said Sikes, seizing the poker in one
hand, and deliberately opening with the other a large clasp-
knife, which he drew from his pocket. *'Come here, you born
devil! Come here! D'ye hear?'*

The dog no doubt heard; because Mr. Sikes spoke in the
very harshest key of a very harsh voice. But, appearing to
entertain some unaccountable objection to having his throat

cut, he remained where he was, and growled more fiercely than before; at the same time grasping the poker between his teeth, and biting it like a wild beast.

This resistance only infuriated Mr. Sikes the more, who dropping on his knees began to assail the animal more furiously. The dog jumped from right to left, and from left to right; SNAPPING, GROWLING, BARKING; the man thrust and swore, and struck and blasphemed; and the struggle was reaching the most critical point for one or other; when the door suddenly opening, the dog darted out: leaving Bill Sikes with the poker and the clasp knife in his hands...

Bill Sikes and Bull's-eye
JOSEPH CLAYTON CLARKE
(1856–1937)

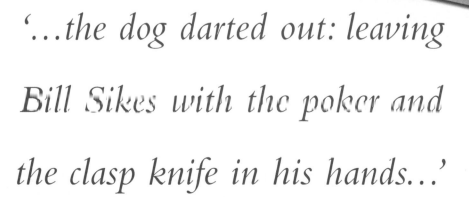

'...the dog darted out: leaving Bill Sikes with the poker and the clasp knife in his hands...'

Beth Gêlert (1898)

by WILLIAM ROBERT SPENCER (1769–1834)

The spearman heard the bugle sound,
And cheerily smiled the morn;
And many a brach, and many a hound
Obeyed Llewellyn's horn.

And still he blew a louder blast,
And gave a lustier cheer,
'Come, Gêlert, come, wert never last
Llewellyn's horn to hear.

'O where does faithful Gêlert roam
The flower of all his race;
So true, so brave – a lamb at home,
A lion in the chase?'

In sooth, he was a peerless hound,
The gift of royal John;
And now no Gêlert can be found
And all the chase rode on.

That day, Llewellyn little loved
The chase of hart and hare;
And scant and small the booty proved,
For Gêlert was not there.

Unpleased, Llewellyn homeward hied,
When near the portal seat,
His truant Gêlert he espied
Bounding his lord to greet.

But when he gained the castle-door,
Aghast the chieftain stood;
The hound all o'er was smeared
  with gore;
His lips, his fangs, ran blood.

Llewellyn gazed with fierce surprise;
Unused such looks to meet,
His favourite checked his joyful guise,
And crouched and licked his feet.

Beth Gêlert (1835)
DANIEL MACLISE (1806–70)
engraved by WILLIAM HENRY MOTE
(fl. 1842–62)

Onward, in haste, Llewellyn passed,
And on went Gêlert too;
And still where'er his eyes he cast,
Fresh blood-gouts checked his view.

O'erturned his infant's bed he found,
With blood-stained covert rent;
And all around the walls and ground
With recent blood besprent.

He called his child
  – no voice replied –
He searched with terror wild;
Blood, blood he found on every side,
But nowhere found his child.

'Hell-hound! my child's by
  thee devoured,'
The frantic father cried;
And to the hilt his vengeful sword
He plunged in Gêlert's side.

Aroused by Gêlert's dying yell,
Some slumberer wakened nigh;
What words the parent's joy could tell
To hear his infant's cry!

Concealed beneath a tumbled heap
His hurried search had missed
All glowing from his rosy sleep
The cherub boy he kissed.

Nor scathe had he, nor harm,
  nor dread,
But, the same couch beneath,
Lay a gaunt wolf, all torn and dead,
Tremendous still in death.

Ah, what was then Llewellyn's pain!
For now the truth was clear;
His gallant hound the wolf had slain,
To save Llewellyn's heir.

Photograph of
Wolfhound (1948)
THOMAS FALL

Greyfriars Bobby
and other Dogs in Mourning

In Shibuya railway station in Tokyo there is a statue to HACHIKO *and thousands of miles away at Fort Benton Station, USA there is another one to* SHEP *– both dogs went every day throughout their lives to the railway stations in the hope of finding their dead masters.*

In Edinburgh there is a little statue to Greyfriars Bobby. The headstone reads '*Greyfriars Bobby – died 14th January 1872 aged 16 years. Let his loyalty and devotion be a lesson to us all.*'

John Gray, with his wife Jess and their son, had moved to Edinburgh in the hope of finding some gardening work. Having had no luck, he joined the police force. It was usual at that time for policemen to be given a watchdog and JOHN'S SKYE TERRIER WAS APPROPRIATELY CALLED BOBBY. A few years later, in 1858, John died of TB and was buried in Greyfriars churchyard. Bobby came to be known as Greyfriars Bobby and for the next 14 years he faithfully watched over the grave.

James Brown, the keeper of the churchyard, had tried to turn Bobby out in the beginning. In the end he gave in and provided him with a bed next to the grave and – along with

other neighbours – made sure he got food and also shelter at night in the winter. Bobby became famous even in his day for his unswerving fidelity. It was none other than the Lord Provost who paid for Bobby's dog licence. He had a collar inscribed for him with the words '*Greyfriars Bobby, from the Lord Provost 1867*'.

The Old Shepherd's Chief Mourner
(c. 1837)
SIR EDWIN HENRY LANDSEER
(1802–73)

'Bobby came to be known as Greyfriars Bobby and for the next 14 years he faithfully watched over the grave'

The Dog and the Reflection

by AESOP (6TH CENTURY BCE)

One day a dog had got hold of a great joint of meat and was carrying it joyfully in his mouth to enjoy it at home in peace. On his way he crossed a log bridge across a running brook. As he did so he happened to look down and caught his reflection in the water. Believing that his reflection was another dog with an even bigger piece of meat than the one he was carrying, he decided to make a grab for it. He snapped at his reflection but as soon as he opened his mouth, of course, the meat fell out and dropped into the waters below. So he was left with nothing. The moral is: BEWARE OF GRASPING AT SHADOWS.

The Fable of the Dog and the Prey
(c. 1653)
PAUL DE VOS (1595–1678)

'Believing that his reflection was another dog with an even bigger piece of meat than the one he was carrying, he decided to make a grab for it'

Spaniel (1866)
PRIVATE COLLECTION

In Memoriam

Now thou art dead, no eye shall ever see
For shape and service spaniel like to thee.
This shall my love do, give thy sad death one
Tear, that deserves of me a million.

UPON HIS SPANIEL TRACEY

by ROBERT HERRICK

Rudyard Kipling was aware that our pets are with us for but a short time, '…the fourteen years which Nature permits', but he still cries out 'why in – Heaven (before we are there)/Should we give our hearts to a dog to tear?' Other expressions of grief are equally touching. Elizabeth Barrett Browning extols the virtues of her companion, Flush: 'This dog watched beside a bed/Day and night unweary.' William Cowper ironically writes of Fop: 'Ye squirrels, rabbits, leverets, rejoice,/ Your haunts no longer echo to his voice.' Sydney Smith wistfully recalls that his 'poor Nick' was 'Of faithful gentle, courteous nature;/A parlour pet unspoilt by favour.'

Exemplary Nick

by SYDNEY SMITH (1771–1845)

Here lies poor Nick, an honest creature,
Of faithful, gentle, courteous nature;
A parlour pet unspoilt by favour,
A pattern of good dog behaviour.
Without a wish, without a dream,
Beyond his home and friends at Cheam,
Contentedly through life he trotted
Along the path that fate allotted;
Till Time, his aged body wearing,
Bereaved him of his sight and hearing,
Then laid him down without a pain
To sleep, and never wake again.

Portrait of a Terrier
(1909)
MONICA GRAY
(fl.1900)

Monica Gray.

Inscription on the Monument of a Newfoundland Dog (1808)

by GEORGE GORDON, LORD BYRON
(1788–1824)

Near this spot
Are deposited the Remains of one

Who possessed Beauty without Vanity,

Strength without Insolence,

Courage without Ferocity,

And all the Virtues of Man, without his Vices.

This Praise which would be unmeaning Flattery

If inscribed over human ashes,

Is but a just Tribute to the Memory of

'Boatswain', a dog,

Who was born at Newfoundland, May, 1803

And died at Newstead Abbey, Nov. 18, 1808.

Newfoundland Dog Called Lion (1824)
SIR EDWIN HENRY LANDSEER
(1802–73)

Fop

by WILLIAM COWPER (1731–1800)

Though once a puppy, and though Fop by name,

Here moulders One, whose bones some honour claim;

No sycophant, although of spaniel race,

And though no hound, a martyr to the chase,

Ye squirrels, rabbits, leverets, rejoice,

Your haunts no longer echo to his voice;

This record of his fate exulting view,

He died worn out with vain pursuit of you.

'Yes!' the indignant shade of Fop replies,

'And worn with vain pursuit Man also dies.'

Dog Guarding
Game (1721)
FRANÇOIS DESPORTES
(1661–1743)

Epitaph to a Dog
by SIR WILLIAM WATSON (1858–1935)

His friends he loved. His fellest earthly foes –

Cats – I believe he did but feign to hate.

My hand will miss the insinuated nose,

Mine eyes that tail that wagged contempt at Fate.

Tray – The Exemplar
by JOHN GAY (1685–1732)

My dog (the trustiest of his kind)

With gratitude inflames my mind;

I mark his true, his faithful way,

And in my service copy Tray.

A Portrait of Shimp (1908)
MABEL F. HOLLAMS
(*fl.*1897–1912)

From To Flush, My Dog (1844)

by ELIZABETH BARRETT BROWNING
(1806–61)

Loving friend, the gift of one
Who her own true faith has run
Through thy lower nature,
Be my benediction said
With my hand upon thy head,
Gentle fellow creature!

Like a lady's ringlets brown,
Flow thy silken ears adown
Either side demurely
Of thy silver-suited breast,
Shining out from all the rest
Of thy body purely.

Darkly brown thy body is,
Till the sunshine striking this
Alchemize its dullness,
When the sleek curls manifold
Flash all over into gold,
With a burnished fullness.

Underneath my stroking hand,
Startled eyes of hazel bland
Kindling, growing larger,
Up thou leapest with a spring
Full of prank and curvetting,
Leaping like a charger.

Pauline Huebner (1829)
JULIUS BENNO HUEBNER
(1806–82)

Yet, my pretty sportive friend,
Little is't to such an end
That I praise thy rareness!
Other dogs may be thy peers
Haply in these drooping ears,
And this glossy fairness.

But of thee it shall be said,
This dog watched beside a bed
Day and night unweary
Watched within a curtained room,
Where no sunbeam brake
  the gloom
Round the sick and dreary.

Roses, gathered for a vase,
In that chamber died apace,
Beam and breeze resigning.
This dog only, waited on,
Knowing that when light is gone
Love remains for shining.

Other dogs in thymy dew
Tracked the hares, and
  followed through
Sunny moor or meadow.
This dog only, crept and crept
Next a languid cheek that slept,
Sharing in the shadow.

Other dogs of loyal cheer
Bounded at the whistle clear,
Up the woodside hieing.
This dog only, watched in reach
Of a faintly uttered speech,
Or a louder sighing.

And if one or two quick tears
Dropped upon his glossy ears,
Or a sigh came double
Up he sprang in eager haste,
Fawning, fondling, breathing fast,
In a tender trouble.

Leap! thy broad tail waves a light,

Leap! thy slender feet are bright,

Canopied in fringes;

Leap – those tasselled ears of thine

Flicker strangely, fair and fine,

Down their golden inches.

Yet, my pretty sportive friend,

Little is't to such an end

That I praise thy rareness!

Other dogs may be thy peers

Haply in these drooping ears,

And this glossy fairness.

And this dog was satisfied

If a pale thin hand would glide

Down his dewlaps sloping

Which he pushed his nose within,

After – platforming his chin

On the palm left open.

Therefore, to this dog will I,

Tenderly, not scornfully,

Render praise and favour;

With my hand upon his head,

Is my benediction said

Therefore and forever.

King Charles Spaniel (1866)
PRIVATE COLLECTION

Kaiser Dead (*c.*1890)

by MATTHEW ARNOLD (1822–88)

What, Kaiser dead? The heavy news
Post-haste to Cobham calls the Muse,
From where in Farringford she brews
The ode sublime,
Or with Pen-bryn's bold bard pursues
A rival rhyme.

Kai's bracelet tail, Kai's busy feet
Were known to all the village street.
'What, poor Kai dead?' say all I meet;
'A loss indeed!'
Oh for the croon pathetic, sweet,
Of Robin's reed!

Six years ago I brought him down,
A baby dog, from London town;
Round his small throat of black and brown
A ribbon blue,
And vouched by glorious renown
A dachshund true.

Cross-Breed Dog (1741)
PRIVATE COLLECTION

His mother, most majestic dame,
Of blood unmixed, from Potsdam came;
And Kaiser's race we deemed the same –
No lineage higher,
And so he bore the imperial name
But ah, his sire!

Soon, soon the days conviction bring.
The collie hair, the collie swing,
The tail's indomitable ring,
The eye's unrest –
The case was clear; a mongrel thing
Kai stood confest.

But all those virtues, which commend
The humbler sort who serve and tend,
Were thine in store, thou faithful friend,
What sense, what cheer!
To us declining tow'rds our end,
A mate how dear!

Thine eye was bright, thy coat it shone;

Thou hadst thine errands off and on;

In joy thy last morn flew; anon,

A fit! All's over;

And thou art gone where Guiot hath gone

And Toss, and Rover.

*Dog Cemetery at
Asnières, France (1908)*
PRIVATE COLLECTION

The Power of the Dog

by RUDYARD KIPLING (1865–1936)

There is sorrow enough in the natural way
From men and women to fill our day;
And when we are certain of sorrow in store,
Why do we always arrange for more?
Brothers and sisters, I bid you beware
Of giving your heart to a dog to tear.

Buy a pup and your money will buy
Love unflinching that cannot lie –
Perfect passion and worship fed
By a kick in the ribs or a pat on the head.
Nevertheless it is hardly fair
To risk your heart to a dog to tear.

When the fourteen years which Nature permits
Are closing in asthma, or tumour, or fits,
And the vet's unspoken prescription runs
To lethal chambers or loaded guns,
Then you will find – it's your own affair –
But... you've given your heart to a dog to tear.

Brizo, a Shepherd's Dog
(1864)
ROSA BONHEUR
(1822–99)

When the body that lived at your single will,

With its whimper of welcome, is stilled (how still!)

When the spirit that answered your every mood

Is gone – wherever it goes – for good,

You will discover how much you care,

And will give your heart to a dog to tear.

We've sorrow enough in the natural way,

When it comes to burying Christian clay.

Our loves are not given, but only lent,

At compound interest of cent per cent.

Though it is not always the case, I believe,

That the longer we've kept 'em, the more do we grieve:

For, when debts are payable, right or wrong,

A short-term loan is as bad as a long –

So why in – Heaven (before we are there)

Should we give our hearts to a dog to tear?

A Portrait of Nettle, a Terrier (1891)
JOHN EMMS (1843–1912)

Picture Credits

Images reproduced with the permission of:

AKG: 11, 43, 55, 80, 91, 117

Bridgeman: 2, 8, 13, 17, 19, 21, 23, 25, 27, 28, 31, 33, 35, 37, 39, 41, 45, 47, 49, 57, 59, 65, 67, 73, 88, 103, 106, 109, 111, 115, 119, 121, 125, 128

Corbis: 7, 15, 51, 53, 60, 63, 75, 76, 87, 105, 127

Mary Evans: 7, 79, 84, 93, 97, 99, 101, 123

Picture Desk: 69, 71, 83, 95, 113